# Learn with Me: Numbers & Counting

**Carson-Dellosa Publishing LLC**
**Greensboro, North Carolina**

# Credits:

Content Editor: Joanie Oliphant

Copy Editor: Sandra Ogle

Layout Design: Lori Jackson

Spectrum
An imprint of Carson-Dellosa Publishing LLC
PO Box 35665
Greensboro, NC 27425 USA
www.carsondellosa.com

Printed in the USA • All rights reserved.
1 2 3 4 5 QUAD 15 14 13 12 11

ISBN 978-1-936024-75-9
335107811

# Table of Contents

Dear Family Member,

Welcome to *Learn with Me: Numbers & Counting*. You and your child are about to start on a new learning adventure. Recent research tells us that the first five years of life is a period of rapid growth in all areas of your child's development. In these years, children develop the basic knowledge, understanding, and interests needed to reach the goal of being successful learners.

*Learn with Me: Numbers & Counting* has been written for families whose children have not yet been to kindergarten. Whether or not your child has attended preschool, kindergarten will be a big change in your child's life. Each day your child learns through play. Perhaps you have observed your child counting his fingers or blocks. Maybe your child has experimented with numbers by counting the number of legs on a kitten or wheels on a car. Your child is naturally building math skills and concepts with play. By working on the activities in this book, you will be helping your child learn more about important math concepts.

This book includes activities that involve sorting, counting, writing, cutting with scissors, and gluing. Some activities are more difficult than others. If your child seems ready for these activities, go ahead with them. But, if your child is not ready, continue to practice with the pages you and your child have completed before moving on to more difficult concepts. For example, on a page where your child should trace a number and write the number word, she can use a finger to trace the number and write it at a later time.

Children practice skills over and over again. For this reason, the pages for the numbers 1 to 10 include making cards for counting practice. Consider gluing the puzzles and games to card stock so your child can use them over and over again.

This is a "togetherness" book. Every activity is meant for families and children to work on together. Preschoolers need your guidance, support, and participation. After all, you are your child's first teacher! As a family member, nothing is better to ensure your child's educational success than spending time together. As you work on the activities in this book, focus on having fun and on the excitement your child feels upon mastering new skills.

Enjoy learning together!

The Spectrum Team

# Zero, Zero, Zero

**Directions:** Read the poem aloud. Talk about the meaning of zero. Trace and color the zero. Cut out the zero. Decorate it.

### Zero

Zero apples,
Zero pudding,
Zero bubblegum
   to chew.
Zero grape juice,
Zero mud pies,
Zero sand grains
   in my shoes.
Zero means that
   there is none.
But, zero is a
   good thing too.
There's zero
   cleanup for me
   to do!!

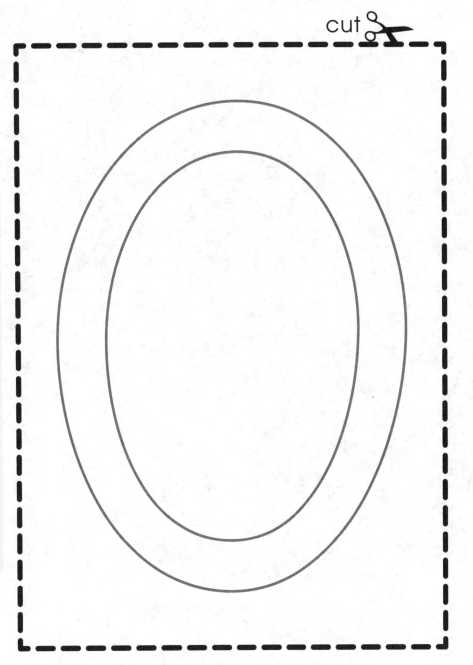

cut

**Directions:** Practice tracing and writing the numbers and the number words on the lines below. Use the blank line for additional practice.

**Directions:** Cut out the cards to use for matching and sequencing.

**Directions:** Practice tracing and writing the numbers and the number words on the lines below. Use the blank line for additional practice.

0 zero

1 one

**Directions:** Cut out the cards to use for matching and sequencing.

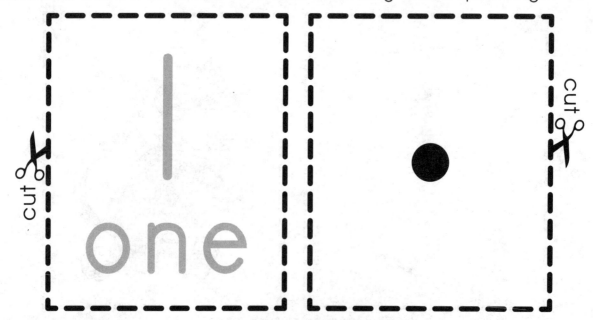

**One Bumblebee**
One, two, three,
I caught a bumblebee!
Three, two, one,
I thought we'd have some fun.
One, two, three,
It flew away from me.
Three, two, one,
I'm glad that it is gone!

**Directions:** Read the poem aloud. Cut out the bees. Glue one bee over the hive. Glue one bee under the hive. Glue one bee on the hive. Glue one bee next to the hive.

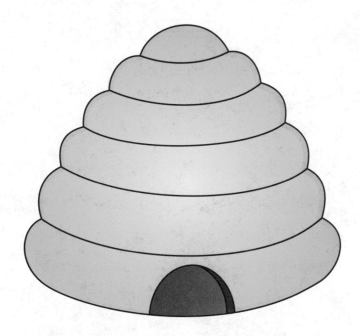

cut

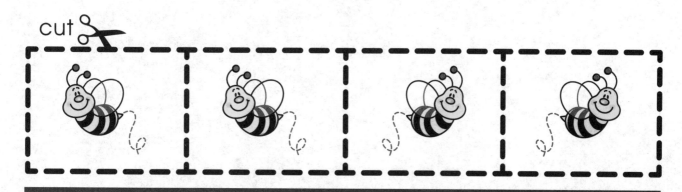

**Directions:** Practice tracing and writing the numbers and the number words on the lines below. Use the blank line for additional practice.

2 2

two two

**Directions:** Cut out the cards to use for matching and sequencing.

2
two

cut

cut

**Directions:** Practice tracing and writing the numbers and the number words on the lines below. Use the blank line for additional practice.

1 one

2 two

**Directions:** Cut out the cards to use for matching and sequencing.

2 two

cut

cut

# Two Cubs Climb a Tree

## Two Bear Cubs

Two bear cubs are playing,
Feeling happy and free.
Then one cub says,
"Let's go climb a tree."

**Directions:** Read the poem aloud. Help the bears find a good climbing tree. Use graham cracker bears as markers. Take turns spinning the paper clip as shown. Move your bear to the next matching space on the path. The first bear to the tree wins!

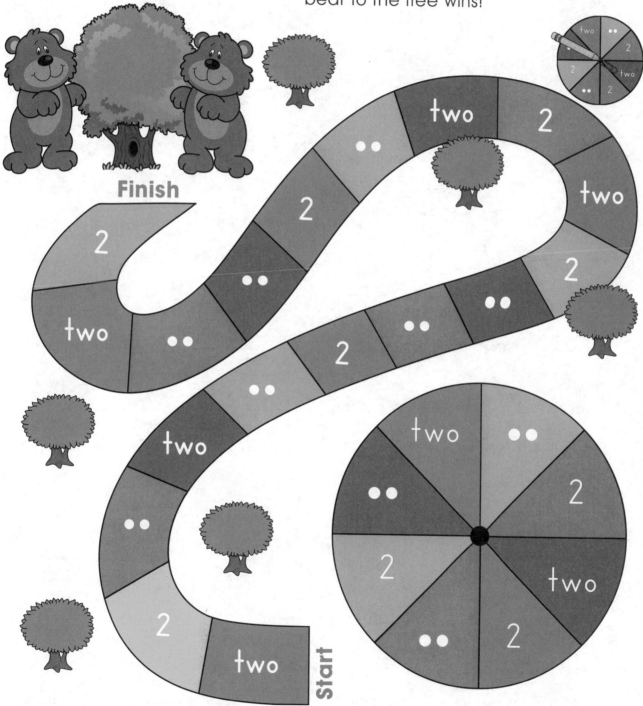

**Directions:** Practice tracing and writing the numbers and the number words on the lines below. Use the blank line for additional practice.

3 3

three three

**Directions:** Cut out the cards to use for matching and sequencing.

cut

3
three

cut

**Directions:** Practice tracing and writing the numbers and the number words on the lines below. Use the blank line for additional practice.

2 two

3 three

**Directions:** Cut out the cards to use for matching and sequencing.

cut ✂

3
three

cut ✂

# Three in the Salad

## My Salad

Three ripe tomatoes,
Three stalks of celery,
Three small onions,
Three large pods of peas.
Three orange carrots,
As tasty as can be.
Three handfuls of lettuce
Make a salad for me!

**Directions:** Read the poem aloud. Cut out the vegetable pictures. Glue them on the salad bowl.

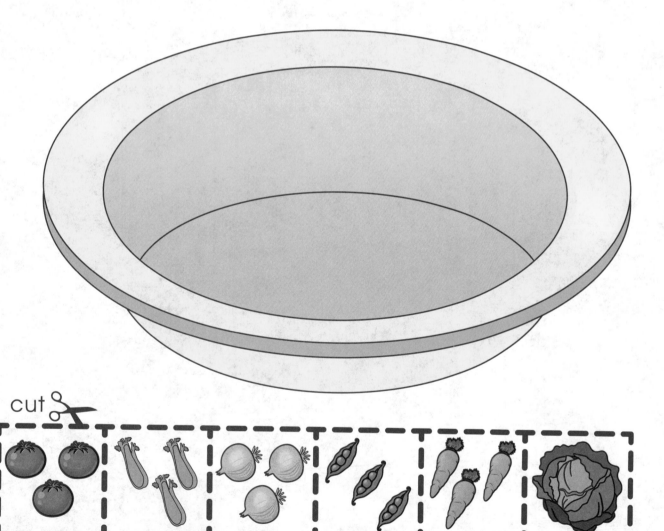

cut ✂

**Directions:** Practice tracing and writing the numbers and the number words on the lines below. Use the blank line for additional practice.

4   4

four   four

**Directions:** Cut out the cards to use for matching and sequencing.

4
four

cut

cut

**Directions:** Practice tracing and writing the numbers and the number words on the lines below. Use the blank line for additional practice.

3 three

4 four

**Directions:** Cut out the cards to use for matching and sequencing.

4 four

cut ✂

cut ✂

## Fours

Four flowers in a vase,
Four birds all in one place,
Four squares on the floor,
Four doorknobs on four doors,
See if you can find the fours,
Then, look around and find
    some more!

**Directions:** Read the poem aloud. Look around your home to find four matching objects of various kinds. Cut out the puzzle. Practice putting it together. Be sure to count the birds, doorknobs, flowers, and floor squares!

cut

**Directions:** Practice tracing and writing the numbers and the number words on the lines below. Use the blank line for additional practice.

5  5

five  five

**Directions:** Cut out the cards to use for matching and sequencing.

5
five

**Directions:** Practice tracing and writing the numbers and the number words on the lines below. Use the blank line for additional practice.

4 four

5 five

**Directions:** Cut out the cards to use for matching and sequencing.

cut

5
five

cut

## My Star Quilt

I have a warm quilt on my bed.
It keeps me snug at night.
It has five stars,
Each has 5 points,
They are colorful and bright!

**Directions:** Read the poem aloud. Count the stars on the quilt. Count the points on the stars. Make a star! Cut out the star center and the triangles. Glue the triangles to the star center.

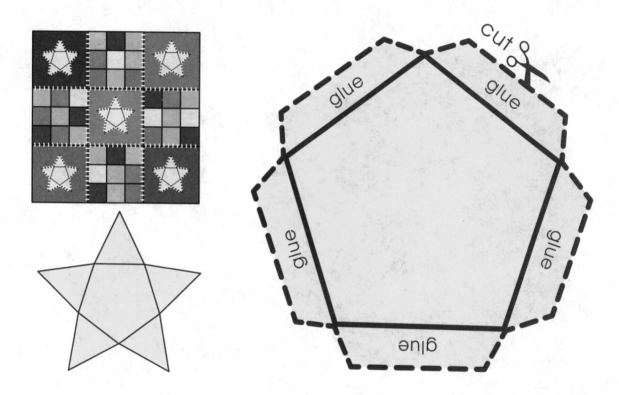

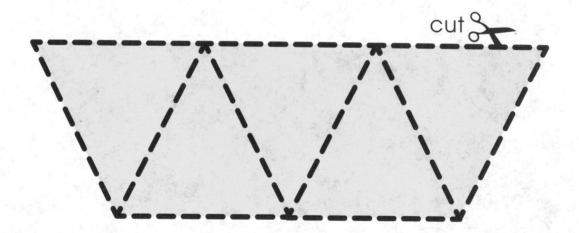

**Directions:** Practice tracing and writing the numbers and the number words on the lines below. Use the blank line for additional practice.

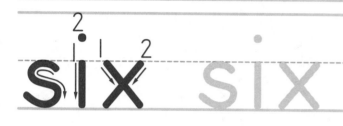

**Directions:** Cut out the cards to use for matching and sequencing.

**Directions:** Practice tracing and writing the numbers and the number words on the lines below. Use the blank line for additional practice.

5 five

6 six

**Directions:** Cut out the cards to use for matching and sequencing.

6 six

cut

cut

**Directions:** Read the tongue twister aloud. Count the chicks and the drums. Cut out the drums. Match the numbers on the drums to the numbers under the chicks. Glue the drums in place.

**Tongue Twister Time**
Six chicks made six quick clicks with six drumsticks.

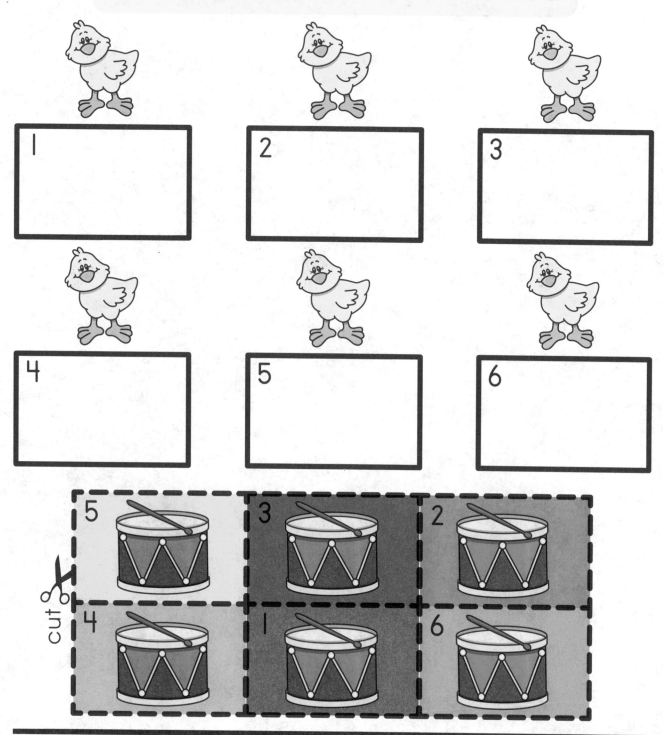

**Directions:** Practice tracing and writing the numbers and the number words on the lines below. Use the blank line for additional practice.

7 7

seven seven

**Directions:** Cut out the cards to use for matching and sequencing.

7

seven

**Directions:** Practice tracing and writing the numbers and the number words on the lines below. Use the blank line for additional practice.

6 six

7 seven

**Directions:** Cut out the cards to use for matching and sequencing.

7 seven

cut

cut

## Rainbow

*(Sing to the tune of "Twinkle, Twinkle Little Star.")*
Rainbow, rainbow way up high,
I love to see you in the sky.
Red and orange, yellow and
   green,
Blue, indigo, and violet are
   seen.
Rainbow, rainbow way up high,
I love to see you in the sky.

**Directions:** Sing the song together. Use the key to color the rainbow. Cut out the color bands. Make a small hole near the top of each band. Arrange the bands in order. Attach them with lengths of ribbon or yarn. Display the mobile in your bedroom window. Use it to practice counting from one to seven.

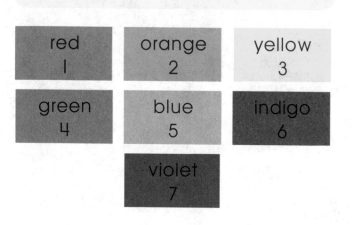

| | | |
|---|---|---|
| red 1 | orange 2 | yellow 3 |
| green 4 | blue 5 | indigo 6 |
| | violet 7 | |

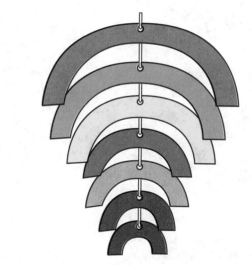

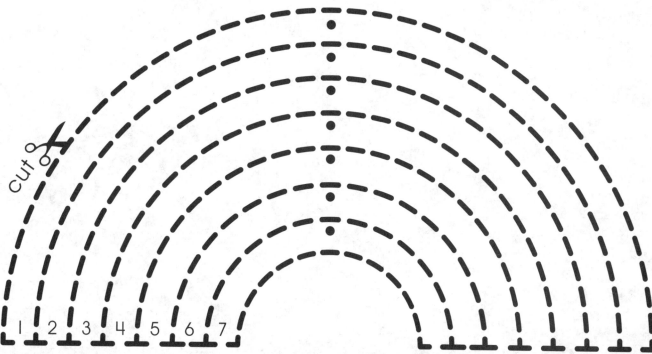

Cut

1 2 3 4 5 6 7

**Directions:** Practice tracing and writing the numbers and the number words on the lines below. Use the blank line for additional practice.

8    8

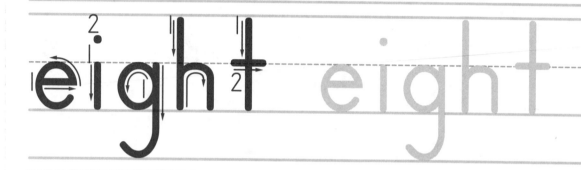    eight

**Directions:** Cut out the cards to use for matching and sequencing.

8
eight

cut

cut

**Directions:** Practice tracing and writing the numbers and the number words on the lines below. Use the blank line for additional practice.

7 seven

8 eight

**Directions:** Cut out the cards to use for matching and sequencing.

8 eight

cut

cut

## My Octopus

My octopus is made from a plate.

Eight arms and a body make her look just great!

What do I like best about my octopus mate?

Her arms wiggle, so I giggle as I count to eight.

One, two, three, four, five, six, seven, eight!

**Directions:** Read the poem aloud. Cut out each octopus arm. Punch eight holes in a paper plate and one hole in each arm. Connect the arms around the plate with brass paper fasteners. Color your octopus. Wiggle each octopus arm as you read the poem aloud again.

1  2  3

4  5  6  7  8

**Directions:** Practice tracing and writing the numbers and the number words on the lines below. Use the blank line for additional practice.

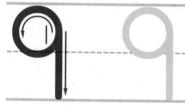

**Directions:** Cut out the cards to use for matching and sequencing.

**Directions:** Practice tracing and writing the numbers and the number words on the lines below. Use the blank line for additional practice.

8 eight

9 nine

**Directions:** Cut out the cards to use for matching and sequencing.

9 nine

# Circus Clown

## Nine Balloons

The circus clown had nine
  balloons,
Red, orange, yellow, green,
  and blue.
She gave one to my sister, and
She gave one to me too!

**Directions:** Read the poem aloud.
Cut out the balloons at the bottom
of the page. Glue a balloon in each
circle. Point to each number. Say its
name.

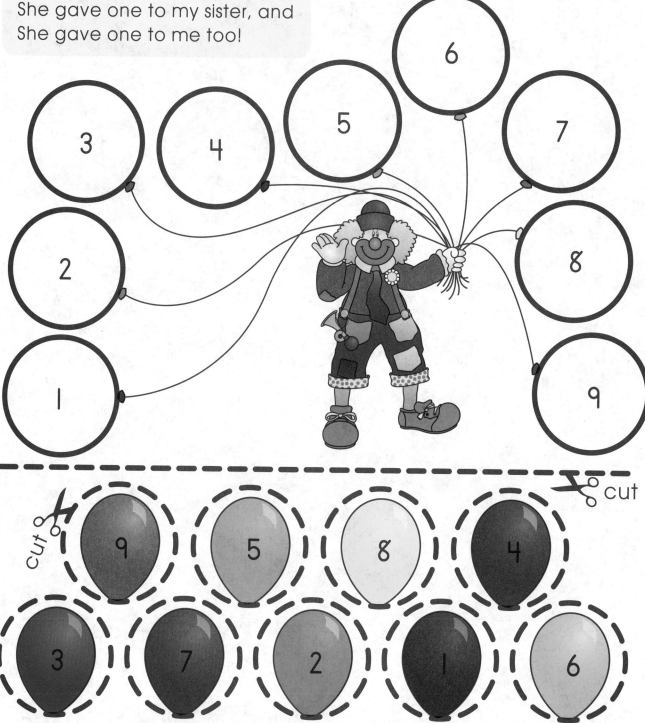

✂ cut

cut ✂

**Directions:** Practice tracing and writing the numbers and the number words on the lines below. Use the blank line for additional practice.

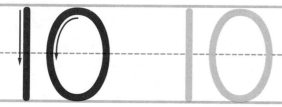

10   10

ten   ten

**Directions:** Cut out the cards to use for matching and sequencing.

10
ten

**Directions:** Practice tracing and writing the numbers and the number words on the lines below. Use the blank line for additional practice.

9 nine

10 ten

**Directions:** Cut out the cards to use for matching and sequencing.

cut ✂

10 ten

cut ✂

# Bend-Hop-Stretch

## Bend-Hop-Stretch

Stretch way up high,
Reach for the sky.
Bend way down low,
Touch all ten toes.
Hop on your left foot,
Then, hop on your right.
Count all the way to ten
Through the day and the night.

**Directions:** Read the poem aloud. Cut out the numbered movement boxes. Glue them on the Bend-Hop-Stretch game board. Use coins as markers. Take turns spinning the paper clip as shown. Move the marker to the matching space on the game board. Bend, hop, or stretch the number of times shown on the space.

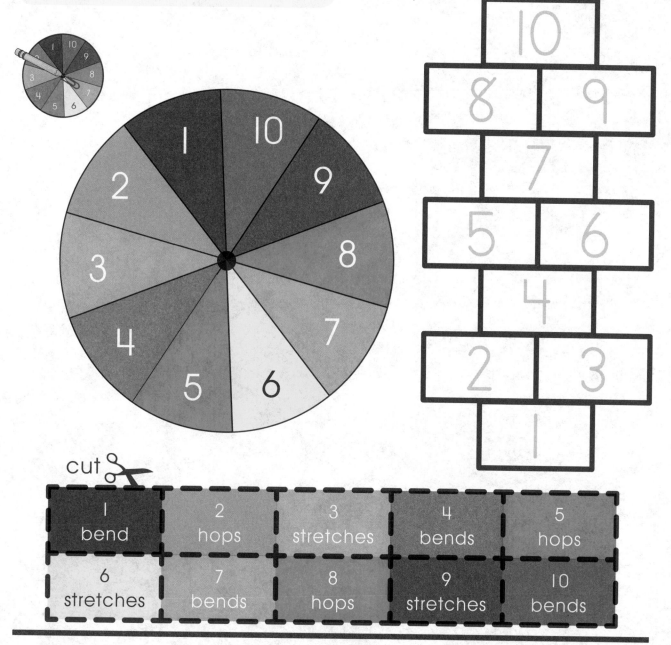

cut

| 1 bend | 2 hops | 3 stretches | 4 bends | 5 hops |
| 6 stretches | 7 bends | 8 hops | 9 stretches | 10 bends |

# 11 Butterflies

**Directions:** Cut out the butterfly wings. Use the patterns and the colors to match the pairs of wings on the 11 butterflies on page 49.

cut ✂

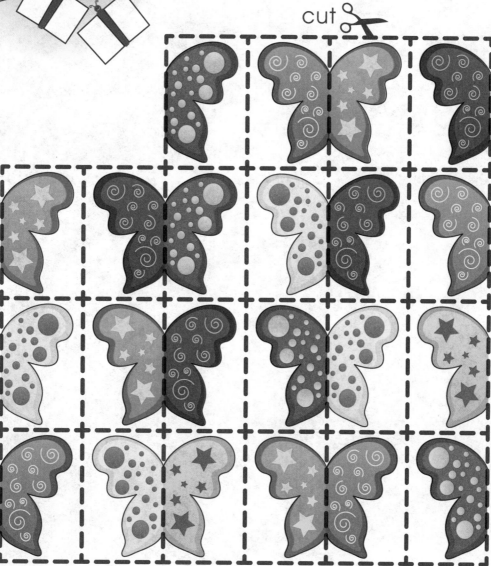

# Match the Butterflies

**Directions:** Glue a pair of matching wings from page 47 to each butterfly body. Count the butterflies.

# 12 Number Clock

**Directions:** Cut out the clock hand and the numbers. Attach the clock hand to the middle of the clock with a brass paper fastener. Glue the numbers in order around the clock. Point the hand to each number to practice counting from 1 to 12.

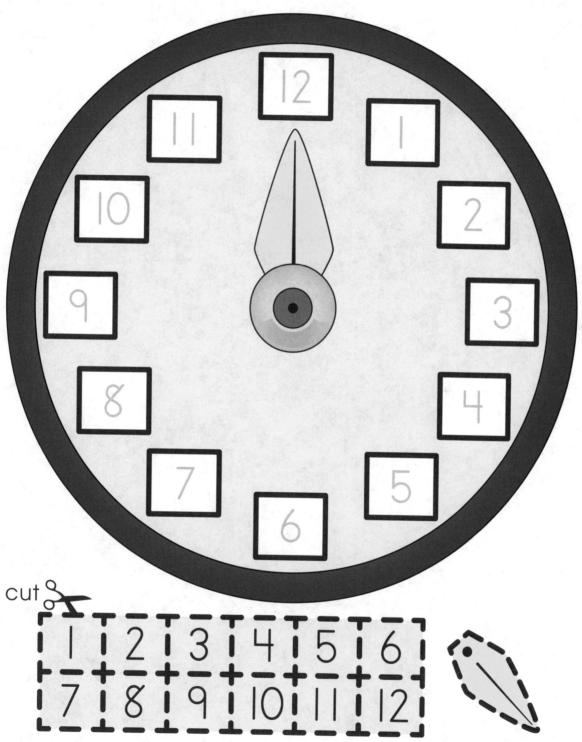

cut

| 1 | 2 | 3 | 4 | 5 | 6 |
|---|---|---|---|---|---|
| 7 | 8 | 9 | 10 | 11 | 12 |

**Directions:** Draw ocean waves on a large sheet of blue construction paper with a crayon or a marker. Cut out the dolphins. Place them in number order on the ocean waves. Glue the dolphins on the construction paper.

cut ✂

**Directions:** Count the 14 bunnies. Cut out the puzzle pieces. Put the puzzle together. Save the puzzle pieces in a resealable plastic bag to use again.

cut ✂

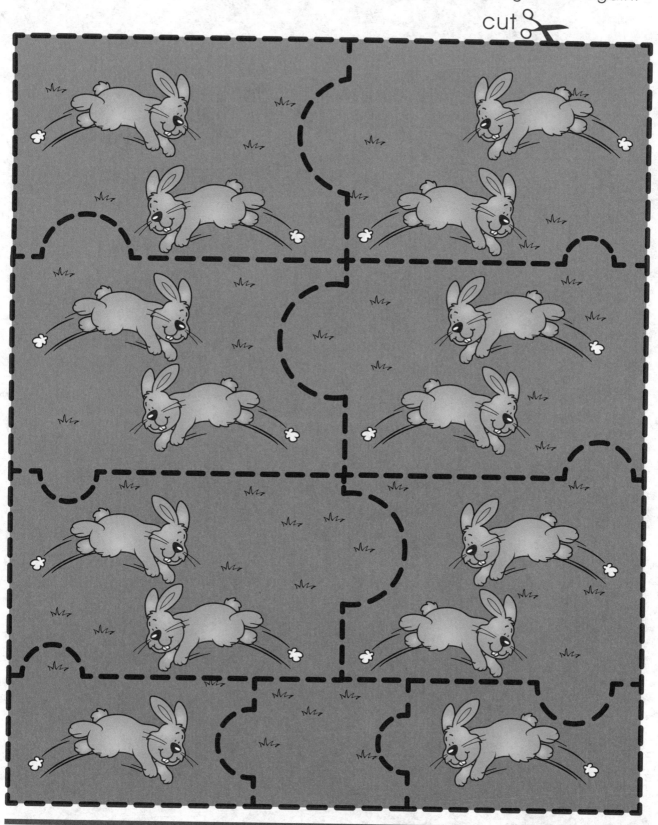

# 15 Keys on a Key Ring

**Directions:** Cut out the keys. Punch a hole at the top of each key. Place the keys in order from 1 to 15. Use a chenille stem or a length of yarn to make a key ring. Use the keys to practice counting from 1 to 15.

cut ✂

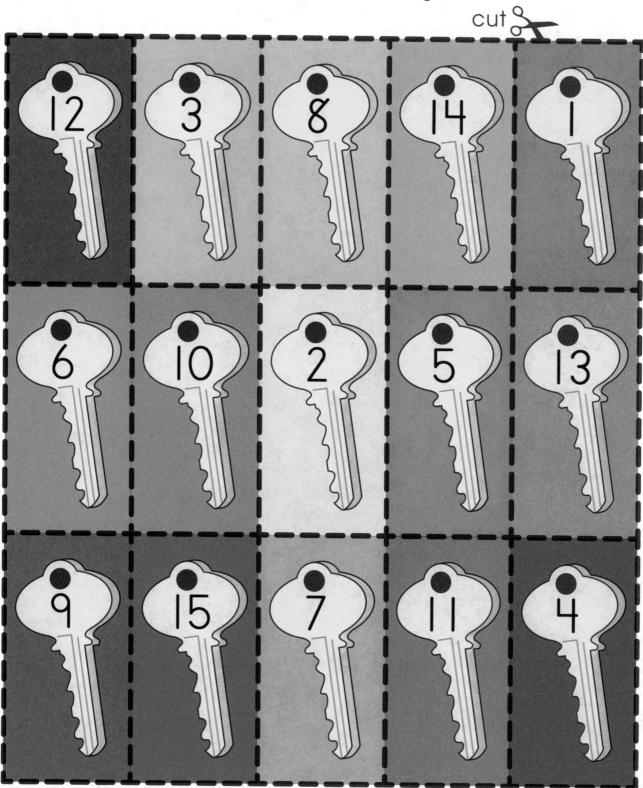

**Directions:** Cut out the anthill picture. With an adult's help, cut 3 sides of each window. Staple the anthill on this page over the anthill on page 61.

cut

**Directions:** Trace the numbers. Staple the anthill with the cutout windows (page 59) on top of this anthill. Open the windows out of order to practice naming the numbers.

# 17 Steps to Treasure

**Directions:** To play, use the spinner on page 45. Take turns spinning the paper clip. Move a coin the number of spaces shown on the spinner. The first player to reach the treasure wins!

**Directions:** To make the 1, cut a 2" x 11" (5 cm x 28 cm) strip of paper. To make the 8, fold two large sheets of gray construction paper in half. With the help of an adult, trace the racetrack pattern on each piece. Cut them out. Overlap the circles to form an 8. Glue the 1 and the 8 onto construction paper as shown.

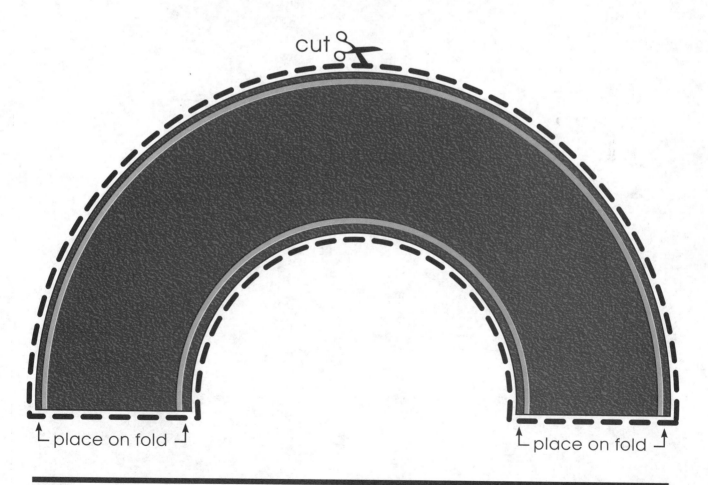

cut

place on fold    place on fold

# 18 Race Cars

**Directions:** Cut out the flags and the race cars. Use the flag pieces to decorate the 1 from page 65. Glue the race cars in order around the 8-shaped track you made on page 65.

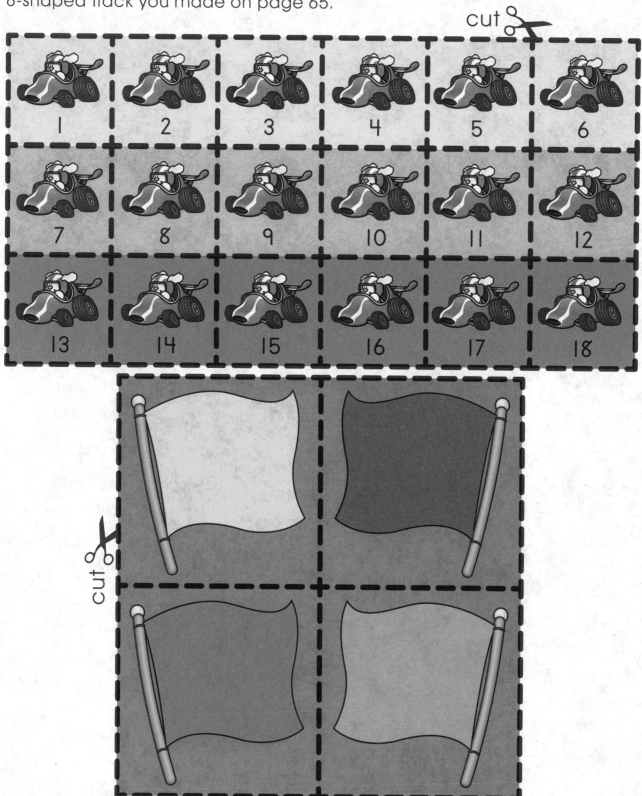

cut ✂

cut ✂

# 19 Counts Home

**Directions:** Cut out the game. Take turns spinning the paper clip. Move a marker, such as a coin, along the path from 1 to 19. A player who makes a wrong move loses a turn. The first player to take the kitten home wins!

cut

# Berry Basket Pattern

**Directions:** Cut out the basket pattern. Fold the two light green horizontal lines. Open the folds. Fold the two light green vertical lines. To finish your basket, follow the directions on page 72.

cut

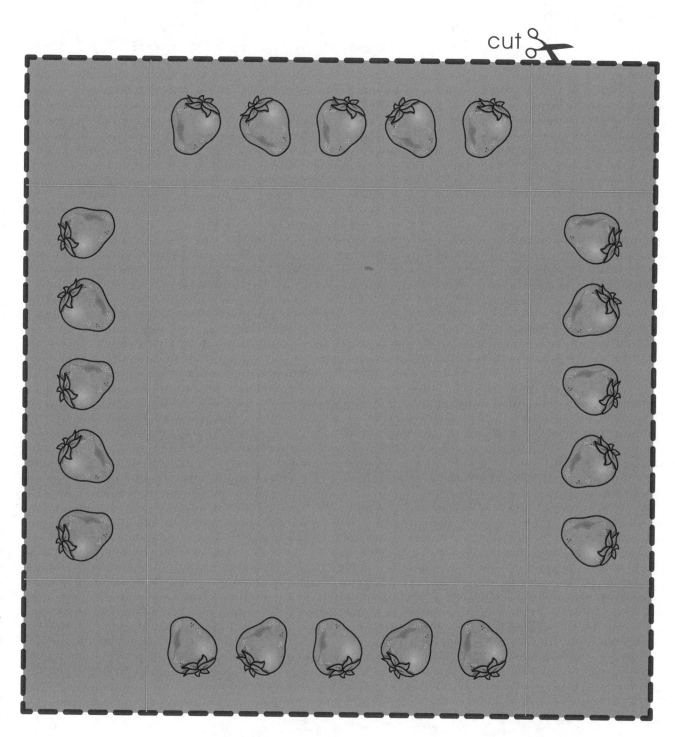

# Berry Basket Pattern

**Directions:** Cut the four marked corners of the basket. Stop at each heavy dot. Bend 1 behind 2. Tape it in place. Bend 3 behind 6. Tape it in place. Bend 9 behind 8. Tape it in place. Bend 7 behind 4. Tape it in place. Your basket is finished!

cut

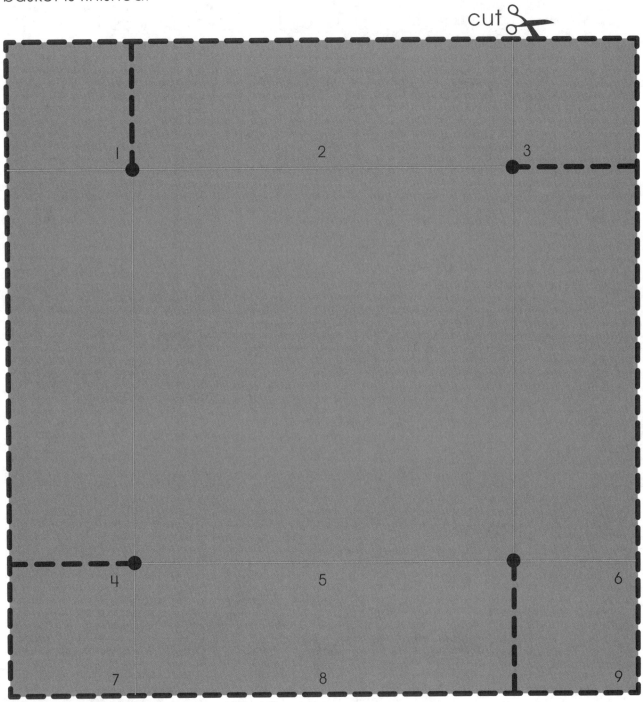

# 20 Berries

**Directions:** Cut out the berries. Mix and place them in the berry basket from page 71. Take out the berries one by one. Tell what the number is.

cut ✂

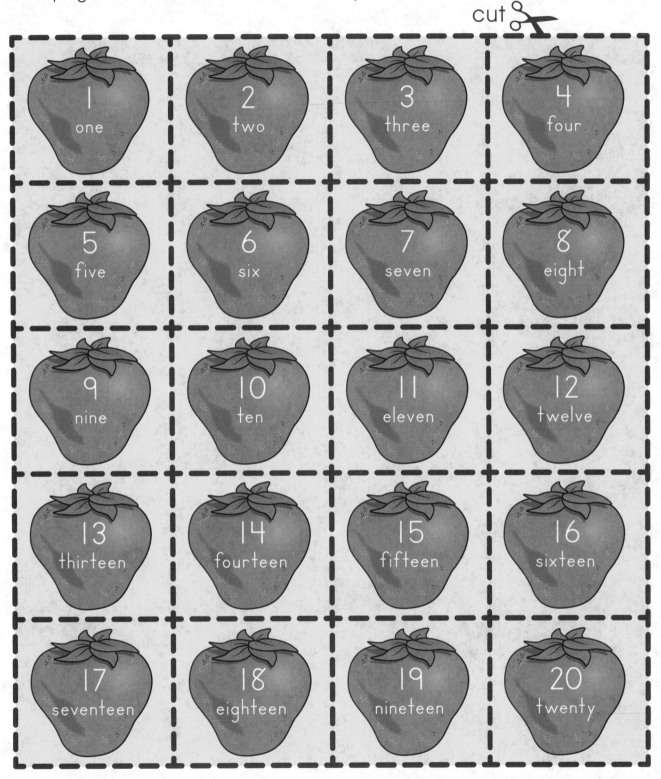

| | | | |
|---|---|---|---|
| 1 one | 2 two | 3 three | 4 four |
| 5 five | 6 six | 7 seven | 8 eight |
| 9 nine | 10 ten | 11 eleven | 12 twelve |
| 13 thirteen | 14 fourteen | 15 fifteen | 16 sixteen |
| 17 seventeen | 18 eighteen | 19 nineteen | 20 twenty |

# Count by Twos

**Directions:** Make this chart to help you practice counting by twos. Cut out the oranges at the bottom of the page. Glue them in order on the chart. Practice reading and saying the numbers on the fruit.

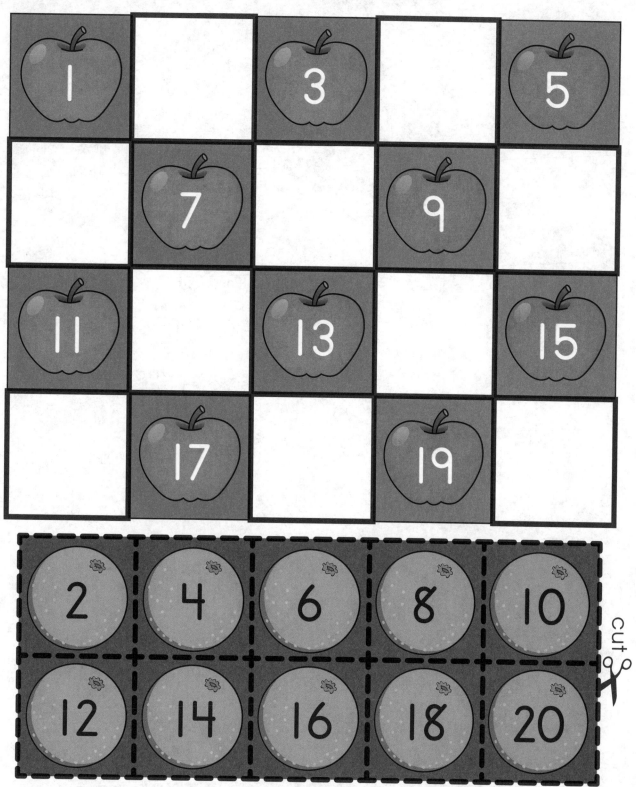

cut

# Count Shoes by Twos

**Directions:** What is a pair of shoes? A pair is two shoes that are the same except they go on different feet! Cut out the shoes. Sort the shoes, putting the pairs in one envelope and the single shoes in another envelope. Count the pairs by twos.

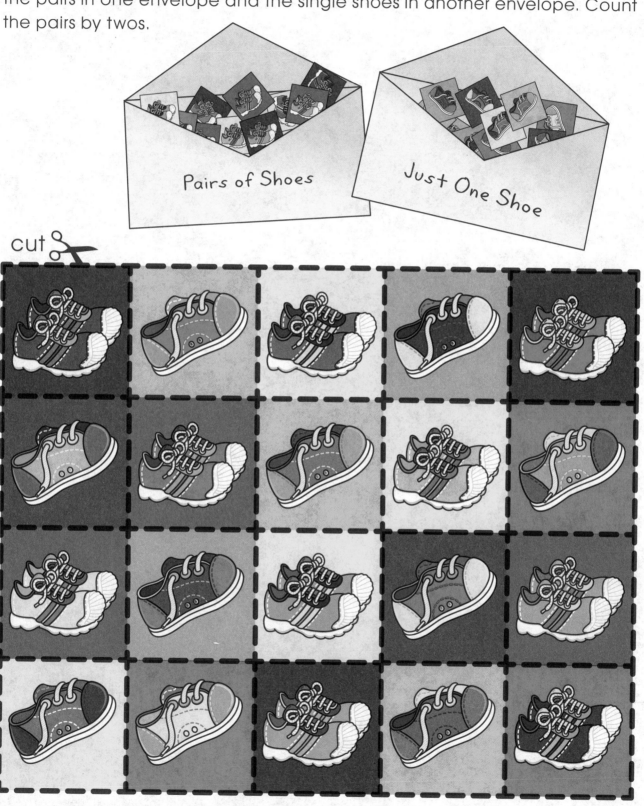

cut ✂

# Counting Rhymes and Songs

Children enjoy learning and reciting rhymes and songs like the ones provided here. As you read and say them together, your child will be reviewing number concepts. In addition, your child will be building important reading skills including the awareness of letters and their sounds, rhyming, and vocabulary.

## One, One, the Zoo Is Lots of Fun

*Author Unknown*

One, one,
The zoo is lots of fun.
Two, two,
See a kangaroo.
Three, three,
See a chimpanzee.
Four, four,
Hear the lions roar.
Five, five,
Watch the seals dive.
Six, six,
A monkey sits on some sticks.
Seven, seven,
The parrot has a red head.
Eight, eight,
A tiger and his mate.
Nine, nine,
Penguins in a line.
Ten, ten,
I want to count again!

## Five Little Monkeys

*Author Unknown*

Five little monkeys jumping on
    the bed.
One fell off and bumped his
    head.
So, Momma called the
    doctor, and the doctor said,
"No more monkeys jumping
    on the bed!"

(Repeat . . .)
Four little monkeys …
Three little monkeys …
Two little monkeys …
One little monkey …

No little monkeys jumping on
    the bed.
None fell off and bumped his
    head.
So, Momma called the
    doctor, and the doctor said,
"Put those monkeys back in
    bed!"

## Over in the Meadow
*Traditional Children's Poem*

Over in the meadow,
In the sand in the sun
Lived an old mother toadie
And her little toadie one
"Wink!" said the mother;
"I wink!" said the one,
So they winked and they blinked
In the sand in the sun

Over in the meadow,
Where the stream runs blue
Lived an old mother fish
And her little fishes two
"Swim!" said the mother;
"We swim!" said the two,
So they swam and they leaped
Where the stream runs blue

Over in the meadow,
In a hole in a tree
Lived an old mother bluebird
And her little birdies three
"Sing!" said the mother;
"We sing!" said the three
So they sang and were glad
In a hole in the tree

Over in the meadow,
In the reeds on the shore
Lived an old mother muskrat
And her little muskrats four
"Dive!" said the mother;
"We dive!" said the four
So they dived and they burrowed
In the reeds on the shore

Over in the meadow,
In a snug beehive
Lived a mother honeybee
And her little bees five
"Buzz!" said the mother;
"We buzz!" said the five
So they buzzed and they hummed
In the snug beehive

Over in the meadow,
In a nest built of sticks
Lived a black mother crow
And her little crows six
"Caw!" said the mother;
"We caw!" said the six
So they cawed and they called
In their nest built of sticks

Over in the meadow,
Where the grass is so even
Lived a happy mother cricket
And her little crickets seven
"Chirp!" said the mother;
"We chirp!" said the seven
So they chirped cheery notes
In the grass soft and even

Over in the meadow,
By the old mossy gate
Lived a brown mother lizard
And her little lizards eight
"Bask!" said the mother;
"We bask!" said the eight
So they basked in the sun
On the old mossy gate

Over in the meadow,
Where the quiet pools shine
Lived a green mother frog
And her little froggies nine
"Croak!" said the mother;
"We croak!" said the nine
So they croaked and they splashed
Where the quiet pools shine

Over in the meadow,
In a sly little den
Lived a gray mother spider
And her little spiders ten
"Spin!" said the mother;
"We spin!" said the ten
So they spun lacy webs
In their sly little den.

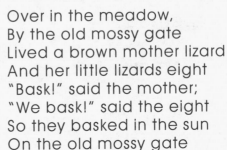

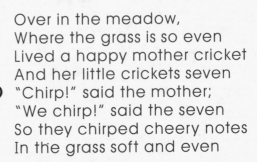